SURVIVING SPIRITUAL BOOT CAMP

EDNA RUTH HOOKER HALL, D. Th.

ISBN 979-8-88955-5131

TABLE OF CONTENTS

ACKNOWLEDGEMENTS

To my husband, Isaac Hall, for his patience. My mom, Hattie Bell Hooker, now deceased, who always told me that I am slow, but I am show. I know she would be so proud of me for accomplishing this milestone in my life.

To my children, Camille, Kevin and Xeniana for their genuine love and support for their on the road Mom. Also, thanks to my spiritual children for stepping up and taking their siblings to places that I couldn't attend. A special thanks to my son-in-law, Willie A. Cooper, Jr who enlightened me about the life of a soldier while going through boot camp. I thank God for the timely visit of Delbert C. Lawrence "Bubba" for sharing his account of survival and thoroughly edited my book without hesitation. Using all resources available to ensure that it was ready for publishing. To Eldress JoAnn Stevens for helping me get my book copyrighted and created my front cover page. Thanks to Keeza Hines for revising my cover page and allowing God to use his gift of designing. To God be all Glory and praise. To Apostle Frederick R. Best and all that assisted him in the publication of this masterpiece.

To my father in the gospel, the late Bishop Ernest O. Edwards who taught me from day one to stay in the word. Live by the word because it will back you when nothing else will. He said the word of God is "Line upon line, and precept upon precept." If you live by it, you will never go wrong. To my elder brother and my mentor Bishop Michael A. Whitfield and Bishop Ronald Mayo, Deans, and professors of the United American FWB Denomination Bible College, for inspiring and encouraging me to give God my best in all that I do. They allowed me to activate the gift of teaching that God instilled within me while

I was a student at the Bible College. After receiving my Doctor of Counseling and Psychology Degree, I became the Dean and instructor of the Snow Hill Satellite Branch of the United American Bible College.

To all my spiritual parents, especially, Pastor Shirley Daniels, (now deceased), Bishop J. E. Reddick, who in 2009 appointed me as one of his Administrative Assistants. To Eldress Ora Kornegay, Eldress Georgia Lewis, Apostle Polly Elliott, and Pastor Agatha Kittrell for loving me and teaching me by example how to live holy and walk in my callings. They always took time out to talk to me no matter when I called them. Each one of them poured into my life in different ways.

To my sisters and brothers, naturally and spiritually for helping me to grow up God's way. Especially to my sister, Geraldine Speight, who is resting with Jesus. She always told me how proud she was of me and kept me encouraged when I wanted to give up and throw in the towel and the bucket. To God I give all glory and praise.

To my sisters and brothers that I gained on November 9, 1973. They accepted me right in and loved me unconditionally. Constantly encouraging me and supporting me in every endeavor.

Tribute to husband, Deacon Isaac Hall who transitioned to be with the Lord before the book was published, but his love for me will never be forgotten. In the 44 years we were married, he would tell me, "Edna Ruth, whatever the Lord tell you to do, DO IT. I got your back and I am with you all the way." He kept every word of it until the day he slipped away, August 24, 2018. I love him for all that he was to me, even when I could not see it. I'm thankful that he didn't throw me away. In his own way he always let me know he loved me and appreciated everything I did for him, even until the end. I love you, "Ike."

DEDICATION

I give honor to God first and foremost for not giving up on me while I was in boot camp. I thank Him for every chance He gave me to get it right, despite of my complaining and murmuring. I am thankful for the prayer warriors God surrounded me with during my going through my throughs. I started writing this book in 2004 but was never able to go any further with getting it published until now. So, this is a revised version of my original. To my husband of 44 years, now deceased, I give special honor. He shared a many of nights sleeping on books, laptops, iPad, and whatever else I needed while I was studying and preparing for this publication. Special thanks go out to the Chara Ministries Deliverance Center Family for believing in me even when they did not understand me or the struggles, I was going through trying to give birth to this baby.

INTRODUCTION

Spiritual boot camp is likened unto a man enrolling in a branch of the United States Armed Services. Jesus oftentimes used parables to help the people get a visual aide of what He was trying to say to them. "Therefore, speak I to them in parables: because they seeing see not; and hearing they hear not, neither do they understand." Matthew 13:13 KJV

According to "TodayMilitary.com" boot camp is also called basic training. They say that this extensive training prepares the incoming recruits for all elements of service (physically, mentally, and emotionally). The article says, "Boot camp will provide the soldiers with the basic tools necessary for them to Military. No matter which branch of the Service a recruit chooses, Basic Training is an intense experience. However, 90 percent complete their first six months of service. The purpose of this training isn't to "break" recruits. In fact, the combination of physical training, field exercises and classroom time makes individuals strong and capable. It's a tough process, but a rewarding one that many services members value for life. The process of surviving boot camp is offered for a duration of 10 weeks. There are things one must do before ever going off to bootcamp. The article makes it specific.

BEFORE BOOT CAMP

"To succeed in boot camp, young adults should prepare themselves physically and mentally. Daily cardio, weight training, push-ups and sit-ups are a must. They should also practice arriving early on a regular basis and sticking to a strict schedule. Finally, potential recruits should delegate personal affairs to family or friends so they can focus on their training. For example, they will need to figure out who will pay the bills, collect the mail, and manage any bank accounts while they are at boot camp." Spiritually you must count up the cost before you make up your mind to enlist in God's army. "Or what king, going to make war against another king, sitteth not down first, and consulteth whether he be able with ten thousand to meet him that cometh against him with twenty thousand?" Luke 14:31 KJV

WHAT NOT TO BRING TO BOOT CAMP

Proper packing can help ease the transition from civilian life to boot camp. The following list of what not to bring can help. Check with a recruiter for a comprehensive list.

Do Not Bring:

- Family Pets
- Expensive personal items – cameras, phones, laptop, jewelry, etc.
- Nonprescription drugs or drug paraphernalia
- Weapons of any type, including pocketknives
- Obscene or pornographic material
- Alcoholic beverages
- Playing cards/dice/dominoes
- Cigarettes/tobacco products

When you decide to follow Jesus, you must be willing to give up life as you know it. "Then said Jesus unto his disciples, "If any man will come after me, let him deny himself, and take up his cross, and follow me." Matthew 16:24 KJV

BOOT CAMP ORIENTATION

While each Branch of Service across the field has different training schedules and requirements, the orientation process is basically the same across Services. During this time, new recruits might:

- Turn in enlistment packages (paperwork from the MEPS)
- Receive dental and medical exams.
- Get immunizations.
- Receive uniforms and training gear (shorts/sweats, T-shirts, etc.)
- Receive required haircuts (women can keep their hair long provided it can be worn within regulation)
- Create direct-deposit accounts for paychecks.

Starting at orientation, the actual training begins. This varies from Service to Service and lasts between eight and 12 weeks. Enrollment is by choice." (The military.com)

At the entrance level of your enlistment God has already done an assessment of you and has given you everything you will need during your stay in boot camp. You will not be operating in your own strength. He will supply all your needs as you need it. All He ask you to do is trust Him as you travel through the process. My son-in-law, Willie Alfice Cooper told me that their officer became their family. He said if their commanding officer could not see a reflection of himself in their shoes, they had to clean them over again.

The stripping process in the spiritual is designed to do the same thing with us. He strips us down or requests that we lay aside and put off our old man until He can see a reflection of himself. Jesus wants to see himself in the way we walk, talk and act. Survival is hard but not impossible. May God's favors be with you as you travel through boot camp to becoming a productive soldier in the army of the Lord. Edna Ruth Hooker Hall, Written 2004 (revised 2017)

CHAPTER ONE

My Journey Through Bootcamp

I was born on December 23, 1954, to the late Hattie Hooker and the late Raymond Wooten. I believe that my spiritual journey began in my mother's womb. My mother was on her way to a party against the wishes of her family, when they had to stop off in Stantonburg, NC, because I would not wait any longer. My mother moved to Washington DC when I was 9 years old. My grandmother, Alice Edwards (Dodge), raised me. She took me to church with her and I learned a lot about Christianity. I did not understand it all, but I continued to go. She passed away in 1967. I was devastated because my grandmother was my heart. I accepted Christ at the age of 9 years old. My journey through spiritual boot camp began immediately. Before my grandmother passed away, she told me that I would have to help raise my sisters and brothers. God was setting me up for active duty. She taught me how to survive as a young child. She taught me how to take care of a household. I cooked, cleaned, and sewed and still excelled in school. I was born with asthma, so, I could not be exposed to extreme heat or cold weather. I worked on the farm after school and sometimes had to stay out of school to pick cotton and cucumbers to help my grandmother feed my siblings. I started driving a school bus at age 16. There were times I did not understand what was going on in my life but I obeyed what I was told to do. I wanted to be like my friends but the yoke of God was so tight on my life until I did not feel comfortable when I was with them. God was setting me apart. Grooming me for active duty. I did get a chance to be a cheerleader when I was in Junior High School. I rode a bicycle three miles back to the school for practices because we did not have a car.

Boot camp prepared me to be able to overcome when I was assigned to go out in the fields. Knowing that there would be times that I would not have a car to ride to church but I was still expected to show up. Going to a movie was considered a sin so I was not allowed to go. I had to make sure, my siblings were taken care of so i did not have time for a social life. Spiritual boot camp for me was hard at times. There were not many of my classmates that were Christians so they did not want me around. They were not mean to me, but I could tell I made them uncomfortable.

Every time I stayed away and tried to be like the other children's bad things would happen to me. I was taught that abstinence was the way to honor God; however, I was sexually abused and molested. I was almost raped three times but God blocked it. I soon learned that when I did not follow the orders of my commander in chief it opened the door for Satan to use me. During my journey I tried to commit suicide because I was tired of being different and taken advantage of. God stepped in and sent the very lady I rode to church with to stop and ask me "why are you walking middle way the road?" I wanted to die. She said, "Don't you know you could get killed?" All I could do was cry. God had a purpose for my life so He would not even let me die. I have learned through my experience that it is easier to be obedient than to try to fit in. Spiritual boot camp conditioned me for active duty.

From the time I preached my initial sermon (1977) until this present day I have practiced everything I learned while going through the process. I have been pastoring 17 years. In boot camp I learned how to use my weapons of warfare (prayer, praise, persistence) instead of fleshy means to win over the enemy. I learned to never put my weapons down. You must be ready "at all times" to combat the enemy. You never know what angle he will be coming but he is coming. He only leaves for a season. I encourage you to allow your time in spiritual boot camp to make you the soldier God knows you can be. "For I know the thoughts that I think toward you, saith the Lord, thoughts of peace, and not of evil, to give you an expected end." Jeremiah 29:11 KJ V

CHAPTER TWO

The Choosing Process

In the natural realm there was a time when people were told that they had to enlist in the army at the age of 18 years old whether they wanted to or not. It did not matter who your parents were or anything else. When you became of age you were expected to enlist. In the spiritual realm the process is very different. You do not just walk in. "No man can come to me, except the Father which hath sent me draw him: and I will raise him up at the last day." John 6:44 KJV

You enlist in God's army at your own free will. "And the Spirit and the bride say, Come. And let him that heareth say, Come. And let him that is athirst come. And whosoever will, let him take the water of life freely. Revelation 22:17 KJV

You Must Be Recruited: The recruiter is Jesus himself. Everyone has the opportunity to receive or reject the invitation to join the army. Jesus's Father never meant that anyone would be lost. "Ye have not chosen me, but I have chosen you, and ordained you, that ye should go and bring forth fruit, and that your fruit should remain that whatsoever ye shall ask of the Father in my name, he may give it you."

John 15:16 "So the last shall be first, and the first last: for many be called, but few chosen." Matthew 20:16 KJV

Joining this spiritual army is easy. Staying in there is difficult because the flesh wants to still do as it has always done. That makes it hard because we will be fighting a spiritual battle. "No man that warreth entangleth himself with the affairs of this life; that he may please him who hath chosen him to be a soldier." 2 Timothy 2:4 KJV

You Must Be Drawn: You always hear people say, I will come to Jesus after a while. What they fail to realize is that after a while may be too late. So many people have been fooled to believe that they have a lot of time left and have died without accepting Christ. "And the Lord said, my spirit shall not always strive with man, for that he also is flesh: yet his days shall be an hundred and twenty years." Genesis 6:3 KJV

Again, I must repeat this verse because satan has fooled so many into believing that they have time wrapped up in their own hand. "No man can come to me, except the Father which hath sent me draw him: and I will raise him up at the last day." John 6:44 KJV

The Entrance Process: There is only one way to enter this army. There is only one Commander in Chief. His name is Jesus. Everyone enters at the same level or rank. Everyone wears the same kind of attire. "Therefore, if any man be in Christ, he is a new creature: old things are passed away;

behold, all things are become new." 2 Corinthians 5:17 KJV

"Verily, verily, I say unto you, He that entereth not by the door into the sheepfold, but climbeth up some other way, the same is a thief and a robber." John 10:1 KJV

"Finally, my brethren, be strong in the Lord, and in the power of his might. Put on the whole armour of God, that ye may be able to stand against the wiles of the devil. For we wrestle not against flesh and blood, but against principalities, against powers, against the rulers of the darkness of this world, against spiritual wickedness in high places. Wherefore take unto you the whole armour of God, that ye may be able to withstand in the evil day, and having done all, to stand. Stand therefore, having your loins girt about with truth, and having on the breastplate of righteousness; And your feet shod with the preparation of the gospel of peace; Above all, taking the shield of faith, wherewith ye shall be able to quench all the fiery darts of the wicked. And take the helmet of salvation, and the sword of the Spirit, which is the word of God:" Ephesians 6:10-17 KJV

Entering God's army is easy but staying in and abiding by the rules may seem to be hard. Paul tells us to endure hardness as a good soldier of Jesus Christ. "Thou therefore endure hardness, as a good soldier of Jesus Christ. No man that warreth entangleth himself with the affairs of this life; that he may please him who hath chosen him to be a soldier." 2 Timothy 2:3-4 KJV.

If you want to make it through boot camp, just follow the orders of the Commander in Chief and be strong. Do not look to the right or to the left. Follow the path that has already been mapped out for you. Jesus knows where all the booby traps are. He will lead you around every one of them. Trust His lead. Do not venture out on your own. Stay with the platoon you have been assigned to. Boot camp will condition you for active battle with the enemy. You will be trained to kill. Your enemy's threefold objective is to take you out at all costs. It does not matter how he does it. "The thief cometh not, but for to steal, and to kill, and to destroy: I am come that they might have life, and that they might have it more abundantly." John 10:10 KJV

You must always be ready for battle. Some you will fight in and some God will say "be at ease, this battle is mine." I interviewed two soldiers who had gone through boot camp around the same time and did not know each other.

CHAPTER THREE

The Accounts of Two Soldiers' Experience Surviving Bootcamp.
Personal Account # 1

Willie Alfice Cooper, my son-in-law was born August 6, 1978. He enlisted in the Army in January 1999. Mr. Cooper served in the United States Army. During his tenure he was deployed to Saudi Arabia during Desert Storm. As they were traveling to their barracks, he watched his best friend get blown away as they followed right behind him in the convoy. He suffers from PTSD from that horrible episode.

His Story: "As far as I remember it all started back in January 1999. I was stationed at Fort Jackson, South Carolina. When I got there it was me and hundreds of other men and women whom I have never seen before. The first people I saw were soldiers dressed in battle dressed uniforms and (BDU'S) shouting and bossing us, the recruits, around; telling us what to do, moving us around, into different groups called platoons. For the next two weeks the platoons went through what is called an initial period. We went through everything from getting shots, to getting our military uniforms, so we could all be the same. After the two weeks we were put on a bus and sent to a remote area where we met the men who were the overseers of us all, the "Drill Sergeants". The first week there is called week 0 or what the Army calls it "hell week." During this time, my platoon went through intense physical tests, otherwise known as PT. Along with the sore muscles and aching feet we were constantly harassed, shouted at, pushed around, and picked on. I guess their motive was to weed out the weak so the strong can step up. As the weeks went by, we went through vigorous training. We did stuff like repelling off a two-story tower. We learned to load and shoot with the M-16 rifle. (The basic line of defense in the Army). We learned how to march and look sharp doing it. We learned how to march and look sharp doing it. We learned how to read a map and to read a compass. We learned how to throw a live grenade. We learned the history of the Army. Other things we learned were how to put on a M-32 gas mask, how to fight using your M-16 weapon and how to use the bayonet. Through all this training we went through several confidence courses where we had to crawl, jump, fall, run, or tiptoe across to succeed. Along with all this training we still had to wake up at 0 dark thirty, in the early morning and run 2, 3, 4, even 5 miles. We had to do a series of push-ups, sit-ups, crunches, etc. Through it all, I, Willie Alfice Cooper, Jr., passed all of the challenges I faced and on that glorious day of graduation I was with the several hundred standing proud and looking good." The End.

Personal Account # 2
Bubba Lawrence

I met Bubba Lawrence by divine connection after praying to God about sending me someone that could connect me with someone that could assist me with paying my husband's medical bills. He is a licensed insurance broker that aids in helping people get the best insurance for their age and financial status. He was truly God sent. He was born August 6, 1981. He enlisted in the Air Force August 3, 1999. How ironic is that? My son-in-law was born August 6, 1978. He enlisted January 1999. I asked Bubba if he would write his version of surviving boot camp. He immediately said yes.

His Story: "Boot camp was a different environment. The majority of us were recently graduated from high school and this was the first time we were away from home. I, however, like most things I chose, excelled well in Boot camp. I knew it was a game of break you down and build you back up. I stayed quiet, did what I was supposed to do and completed it with no issues. One of my most memorable experiences was completing the monkey bars over the lake. I have never completed a monkey bars' course, ever.

CHAPTER FOUR

The Stripping Process

To strip means to take off something. In the army, the soldiers had to take off everything and anything that reminded them of their past life. (From their head to their feet)

The process of stripping off is designed to help the newborn babes in Christ to develop a lifestyle of dependence on God. This process also aids the matured Christian to continue to separate themselves from the things of the world that will hinder or stunt their growth. Paul says, "Therefore if any man be in Christ, he is a new creature: old things are passed away; behold, all things are become new."2 Corinthians 5:17 KJV The passing away of old things deal with the stripping off the old life. The old man must die. You grow as you go. You live as you learn. Jesus said, take my yoke upon you and learn of me, for I am meek and lowly in heart; and ye shall find rest unto your souls. For my yoke is easy and my burdens are light. (Mat. 11:29-30) When you feel the load getting heavy remind yourself of whose yoke you are supposed to be carrying. God cannot and will not lie. As you take on His yoke the mortification process begins.

Mortify is the root word of mortification. It means to kill off or pull off. It is the first step of the stripping process. Putting on is the second step of the process. Pulling off and putting on completes the stripping process. We were all born in sin and shaped in iniquity according to Ps. 51:5. We all have sinned and come short of the glory of God. Rom. 3:23. For you to become the disciple that you were created to be you must go through the process. "Mortify therefore your members which are upon the earth; fornication, uncleanness, inordinate affection, evil concupiscence, and covetousness, which is idolatry: But now ye also put off all these; anger, wrath, malice, blasphemy, filthy communication out of your mouth. Lie not one to another, seeing that ye have put off the old man with his deeds;" Colossians 3:5, 8-9 KJV

"You did not put on all of this in one night or day and you will not put it all off in one or two days. Also, we are told by Paul that "Wherefore seeing we also are compassed about with so great a cloud of witnesses, let us lay aside every weight, and the sin which doth so easily beset us, and let us run with patience the race that is set before us," Hebrews 12:1 KJV

How will you know you are ready for active duty? Your officer in command will be the one to say you have passed all necessary requirements to move further. Paul said, "When I was a child, I spake as a child, I understood as a child, I thought as a child: but when I became a man, I put away childish things." 1 Corinthians 13:11 KJV

Another translation says, "When I was an infant at my mother's breast, I gurgled and cooed like any infant. When I grew up, I left those infant ways for good." 1 Corinthians 13:11 MSG

You may have enlisted as a child, but by the time they have finished with you, you have put away those childish ways.

CHAPTER FIVE

The Redressing Process

(Put some clothes on)

As stated in the previous chapter, the process of stripping took you through a taking off the old man and its deeds. Just like you cannot walk around naked lawfully in the natural, you can not walk around naked in the spiritual. You have got to put some clothes on. Humble yourself and let God clothed you. Little babies have no shame. They love to run around with no clothes on. They are not conscious of the fact that being naked in public is wrong. "Likewise, ye younger, submit yourselves unto the elder. Yea, all of you be subject one to another, and be clothed with humility: for God resisteth the proud, and giveth grace to the humble." 1 Peter 5:5 KJV.

When you allow yourself to be naked, you open yourself up for satan to have his way with you. Satan is always lurking around to attack you. Matthew warns you in the scriptures. He says, "When the unclean spirit is gone out of a man, he walketh through dry places, seeking rest, and findeth none. Then he saith, I will return into my house from whence I came out; and when he is come, he findeth it empty, swept, and garnished. Then goeth he, and taketh with himself seven other spirits more wicked than himself, and they enter in and dwell there: and the last state of that man is worse than the first. Even so shall it be also unto this wicked generation." Matthew 12:43-45 KJV

Another translation says it this way. "When a defiling evil spirit is expelled from someone, it drifts along through the desert looking for an oasis, some unsuspecting soul it can bedevil. When it doesn't find anyone, it says, 'I'll go back to my old haunt.' On return it finds the person spotlessly clean, but vacant. It then runs out and rounds up seven other spirits eviler than itself and they all move in, whooping it up. That person ends up far worse off than if he'd never gotten cleaned up in the first place. "That's what this generation is like: You may think you have cleaned out the junk from your lives and gotten ready for God, but you weren't hospitable to my kingdom message, and now all the devils are moving back in." Mat. 12:43-45 MSG

It is important to fill that empty space from which you were delivered with "God stuff. "And be not drunk with wine, wherein is excess; but be filled with the Spirit; Speaking to yourselves in psalms and hymns and spiritual songs, singing and making melody in your heart to the Lord;" Ephesians 5:18-19 KJV

"You must guard yourself from head to toe, from the inside out so satan cannot get to you. He desires to "sift you as wheat" Luke 22:31.

He starts as soon as you make the confession. His goal is to steal your confession and destroy or kill you as soon as possible. John 10:10.

John 1:12 tells us that when you come to him, He gives you power to become the sons of God. You cannot do it on your own.

It is in Him that we live, move, and have our being. "Acts 17:28.

In order to be successful you have to follow the instructions in Colossians. "And have put on the new man, which is renewed in knowledge after the image of him that created him: Put on therefore, as the elect of God, holy and beloved, bowels of mercies, kindness, humbleness of mind, meekness, longsuffering; Forbearing one another, and forgiving one another, if any man have a quarrel against any: even as Christ forgave you, so also do ye. And above all these things put on charity, which is the bond of perfectness." Colossians 3:10, 12-14 KJV

You must put on the whole armor of God so that you can fight an effective fight against the enemy. You must be clothed with righteousness in order to survive spiritual boot camp. Put the garment of praise on so that you will be able to rejoice when you are not understood. Jesus was anointed for such a time as this. He was anointed "To appoint unto them that mourn in Zion, to give unto them beauty for ashes, the oil of joy for mourning, the garment of praise for the spirit of heaviness; that they might be called trees of righteousness, the planting of the Lord, that he might be glorified." Isaiah 61:3 KJV

Spiritual boot camp requires having your mind renewed. If your mind is not renewed, you will not be able to lay aside every weight and sin that try to hinder you from running your race. Your mind will keep reverting to how you used to do things; especially when things do not go your way. Paul wrote, "I beseech you therefore, brethren, by the mercies of God, that ye present your bodies a living sacrifice, holy, acceptable unto God, which is your reasonable service. And be not conformed to this world: but be ye transformed by the renewing of your mind, that ye may prove what is that good, and acceptable, and perfect, will of God." Romans 12:1-2 KJV

My husband told me of a time he did not want to do as he was instructed while he was in the army. He soon found out, the hard way, that being haughty was a bad move. You cannot tell your Commanding Officer what you are or are not going to do without severe consequences. Haughtiness does not make you a good soldier naturally or spiritually. You must be willing to take orders. You must check your surroundings and realize you are not at Burger King. `You cannot have it your way. Your steps are now ordered by the Lord, and you must follow them if you want to make it through boot camp. "Ps. 37:23. Spiritual Boot camp helps rid you of unhealthy pride and haughtiness. Pride is one of the seven things God hates. Pride comes before destruction. "Pride goeth before destruction, and a haughty spirit before a fall." Proverbs 16:18 KJV

"Before destruction the heart of man is haughty, and before honour is humility." Proverbs 18:12 KJV

You go further in life being humble. "Likewise, ye younger, submit yourselves unto the elder. Yea, all of you be subject one to another, and be clothed with humility: for God resisteth the proud, and giveth grace to the humble. Humble yourselves therefore under the mighty hand of God, that he may exalt you in due time:"1 Peter 5:5-6 KJV Your flesh will dictate to you another message. It will say you are being used, mistreated, or picked on and you do not have to take this kind of treatment. Paul said, "For I delight in the law of God after the inward man: But I see another law in my members, warring against the law of my mind, and bringing me into captivity to the law of sin which is in my members." Romans 7:22-23 KJV

CHAPTER SIX

Survival Techniques

Survival is the focus while you are in boot camp. The vigorous exercises and routines you must encounter will increase your desire to survive. In order to survive spiritual boot camp there are some things you must do intellectually. Doing things intellectually means acting on intellect not emotions and feelings. To do this you must exercise the following steps.

- **Have the right mindset:** Set your mind on Christ. Become God Conscious. "Thou wilt keep him in perfect peace, whose mind is stayed on thee: because he trusteth in thee. Isaiah 26:3 KJV

- **Set your mind on things above not on this earth:** "If ye then be risen with Christ, seek those things which are above, where Christ sitteth on the right hand of God. Set your affection on things above, not on things on the earth." Colossians 3:1-2 KJV Get your mind away from those collards, potatoes, fried chicken, and pork chops and accept that army food with a smile.

- **Be transformed by the renewing of your mind.** Allow the training to reshape your thoughts so you can be the best that God has called you to be. And be not conformed to this world: but be ye transformed by the renewing of your mind, that ye may prove what is that good, and acceptable, and perfect, will of God." Romans 12:2 KJV "That ye put off concerning the former conversation the old man, which is corrupt according to the deceitful lusts; And be renewed in the spirit of your mind;" Ephesians 4:22-23 KJV. Allow the process to transform you into a real soldier of the cross.

You must present your bodies as living sacrifices: Give yourself away to Jesus. Let him rule your whole mind. "I beseech you therefore, brethren, by the mercies of God, that ye present your bodies a living sacrifice, holy, acceptable unto God, which is your reasonable service."Romans 12:1 KJV

Ask for directions before you do anything. Begin, continue, and end every work, purpose, and plan with God. Self-sufficiency and self-confidence have been the ruin of mankind ever since the fall. Man's sin has been to live independently of God. True religion consists of full acknowledgement of God in all human affairs. "In all thy ways acknowledge him, and he shall direct thy paths." Proverbs 3:6 KJV.

- Lay down everything so you can run this race effectively: Forsake everybody and everything. Be strong, courageous and follow directions. If you do not follow directions, you will not survive spiritual boot camp. You stand a chance of getting rejected. Saul was rejected because he did not follow directions. He got caught up in his selfish pride and started lying. Lying led to him trying to murder David. Heb. 12:1

CHAPTER SEVEN

Penning of Awards

Surviving spiritual boot camp is a rewarding accomplishment. Anything you start for the first time; you are a baby in it. We are admonished to desire the sincere milk of the word when we first become saved. 1 Peter 2:2.

Boot camp continues until you are conditioned to go into active battle. It was stated in a survey that you keep doing it over and over until you get it right. If they see that you just are not cut out for it you are discharged as unfit for service. According to Google search there are thirteen ranks in the U. S. Army. Private, Private First Class, Specialist, Corporal, Sergeant, Staff Sergeant, Sergeant First Class, Master Sergeant, First Sergeant, Sergeant Major, Command Sergeant Major, and Sergeant Major. These are broken down into three groups. Junior,

NCOs, and Senior NCOs. In the army of God, we have babes needing milk and those of full age needing strong meat. US Army Ranks states that when you come into the army via basic training (boot camp) your rank depends on what you have accomplished before enlisting. By default, the article says you enter as an E-1 (Private). By default, you enter the body of Christ as a son of God, a new creature, a babe. No matter how much

knowledge you have acquired or degrees you have obtained, you still have the same rank. I talked to a young man by the name of Domonic Powell and he told me that at the end of boot camp you have a graduation/award ceremony. After the ceremony you are sent to a school of further training for your military job. This army that we have enlisted in has great benefits. Boot camp prepares you for the real war. The war we are fighting is not with flesh and blood but spiritual. "For though we walk in the flesh, we do not war after the flesh: (For the weapons of our warfare are not carnal, but mighty through God to the pulling down of strong holds;)" 2 Corinthians 10:3-4 KJV. There will be an award ceremony when you are done warring in this spiritual war. "But he that shall endure unto the end, the same shall be saved." Matthew 24:13 KJV "Blessed is the man that endureth temptation: for when he is tried, he shall receive the crown of life, which the Lord hath promised to them that love him." James 1:12 KJV

CHAPTER EIGHT

Declaration of a Good Soldier

It is a rewarding thing for a soldier to graduate from boot camp, serve in the military and come back home to his family. To declare means to make something known or clear. There is no greater reward than for a soldier to be saluted at the end of a tenure at war and be pinned for their time served. Paul said at the end of his tenure in this spiritual war, "I have fought a good fight, I have finished my course, I have kept the faith:" 2 Timothy 4:7 KJV

At the end of this war, you are fighting it will be a welcoming reward to hear God say that He is pleased with the way you have carried yourselves. Matthew said, "And so he that had received five talents came and brought other five talents, saying, Lord, thou deliveredst unto me five talents: behold, I have gained beside them five talents more. His lord said unto him, Well done, thou good and faithful servant: thou hast been faithful over a few things, I will make thee ruler over many things: enter thou into the joy of thy lord." Matthew 25:20-21 KJV

All of us that have accepted the call to salvation are looking forward to hearing our Savior say those welcoming words. It has been promised to all of those that believe. It is not how fast you run the race that is important, but that you finish the race strong. "I returned, and saw under the sun, that the race is not to the swift, nor the battle to the strong, neither yet bread to the wise, nor yet riches to men of understanding, nor yet favour to men of skill; but time and chance happeneth to them all." Eccl. 9:11 KJV

"Thou therefore endure hardness, as a good soldier of Jesus Christ." 2 Timothy 2:3 KJV teaches us a lesson in endurance. It is not going to be easy, but it will be worth it. So, strive for the mastery. "And every man that striveth for the mastery is temperate in all things. Now they do it to obtain a corruptible crown; but we an incorruptible." 1 Corinthians 9:25 KJV

The Dakes Annotated Study Bible notes on this scripture says, "Just as a good soldier lives up to certain standards, an athlete obeys the rules of the game to win, and a farmer tills according to natural laws of agriculture to get a crop, so the minister must live up to the rules if he expects a crown and eternal fruit."

I hope that after reading this book you will have been enlightened and encouraged to stay on the battlefield for the Lord. No matter what happens in your life, nothing is worth turning around and going back. The Bible says, "And Jesus said unto him, No man, having put his hand to the plough, and looking back, is fit for the kingdom of God." Luke 9:62 KJV

If you are reading this book and you have not made a commitment to Christ, I invite you to accept Him now as your personal Savior. Allow Jesus to take complete control of your life. As you enter spiritual boot camp, allow Jesus to lead you through and you will come out with honors. If you were once a soldier and for whatever reason has left the army (gone AWOL), I invite you to reconsider and come back. Jesus is waiting for you. "Wherefore, as by one man sin entered into the world, and death by sin; and so death passed upon all men, for that all have sinned:" Romans 5:12 KJV.

You are not the only one. "For all have sinned and come short of the glory of God;" Romans 3:23 KJV.

He is calling right now for recruiters, do not be like the foolish that was invited to the wedding but would not come. They had so many excuses. "And sent forth his servants to call them that were bidden to the wedding: and they would not come. Again, he sent forth other servants, saying, tell them which are bidden, Behold, I have prepared my dinner: my oxen and my fatlings are killed, and all things are ready: come unto the marriage. But they made light of it, and went their ways, one to his farm, another to his merchandise:" Matthew 22:3-5 KJV.

Accept His offer for eternal life today. The plan of salvation is as simple as learning the ABCs.

1. **Acknowledge**: Acknowledge means to admit that what you are saying is true. "Have mercy upon me, O God, according to thy lovingkindness: according unto the multitude of thy tender mercies blot out my transgressions. Wash me thoroughly from mine iniquity and cleanse me from my sin. For I acknowledge my transgressions: and my sin is ever

before me. Against thee, thee only, have I sinned, and done this evil in thy sight: that thou mightest be justified when thou speakest, and be clear when thou judgest. Behold, I was shapen in iniquity; and in sin did my mother conceive me. Behold, thou desirest truth in the inward parts: and in the hidden part thou shalt make me to know wisdom. Purge me with hyssop, and I shall be clean: wash me, and I shall be whiter than snow. Make me to hear joy and gladness; that the bones which thou hast broken may rejoice. Hide thy face from my sins and blot out all mine iniquities. Create in me a clean heart, O God; and renew a right spirit within me. Cast me not away from thy presence; and take not thy holy spirit from me. Restore unto me the joy of thy salvation; and uphold me with thy free spirit." Psalms 51:1-12 KJV

2. **Believe**: To accept something as true. "That if thou shalt confess with thy mouth the Lord Jesus, and shalt believe in thine heart that God hath raised him from the dead, thou shalt be saved." Romans 10:9 KJV "For God so loved the world, that he gave his only begotten Son, that whosoever believeth in him should not perish, but have everlasting life." John 3:16 KJV.

3. **Confess**: Admit or acknowledge something. "If we confess our sins, he is faithful and just to forgive us our sins, and to cleanse us from all unrighteousness." 1 John 1:9 KJV.

Now that you have made your confession and accepted the Lord as your Lord and Savior, find yourself a church that teaches the word of God. Study the word daily and apply it to your life. Jesus will never leave you or forsake you. "Trust in the Lord with all thine heart; and lean not unto thine own understanding. In all thy ways acknowledge him, and he shall direct thy paths. Be not wise in thine own eyes: fear the Lord and depart from evil. It shall be health to thy navel, and marrow to thy bones." Proverbs 3:5-8 KJV

Spiritual boot camp began the moment you enlisted into the army of the Lord. Your life became brand new. Stay the course and you will make God a good soldier. "Therefore, if any man be in Christ, he is a new creature: old things are passed away; behold, all things are become new." 2 Corinthians 5:17 KJV.

ABOUT THE BOOK

Surviving Spiritual Boot Camp is a concise book on how to maintain your walk with Christ during the trials, tribulations, testing, and temptations. It will guide you through the pitfalls all of us encounter when we enter the war against the enemy. It will discuss strategies that will help you combat the wiles of the devil and engage in effective warfare that we are all confronted with as Christians. We are told that we are not ignorant of the devil's devices, so we will learn how to war in the spirit realm against the enemy. For the weapons of our warfare are not carnal, but mighty unto God to the pulling down of strongholds. Our weaponry is spiritual. We must fight spirit with spirit. Surviving Spiritual Bootcamp is a necessary tool for anyone that is seeking to enter this war or is already in this war against the devil. Get your copy today.

ABOUT THE AUTHOR

I was born December 23, 1954, to the late Hattie Bell Hooker and the late, Raymond Wooten. Raised with 7 other siblings by my grandmother and mother. Eight was enough. I was married 44 years to the late Isaac Hall, and we have 3 children. I had been pastoring Chara Ministries Deliverance Center for over 17 years at the time this book was authored. Boot camp for me started when I was 6 years old. As a child I knew nothing about spiritual warfare, therefore I spent a lot of time failing, falling, and fainting. God took me through boot camp and trained me how to stand against opposition. I experienced a lot of traumatic setbacks that made me want to quit but there was something inside of me that kept telling me to press on. There were times I thought God was punishing me, but I learned that He was just preparing me for the real battle. Preparation Proceeds Proclamation. The battle was real. Your whole being is put on display for the enemy to take shots at, but God continuously reminded me that He was with me and that He would never leave me.